I0410751

SRI LANKA'S DEMOCRATIC TRANSITION: A NEW ERA FOR THE U.S.-SRI LANKA RELATIONSHIP

HEARING

BEFORE THE

SUBCOMMITTEE ON ASIA AND THE PACIFIC

OF THE

COMMITTEE ON FOREIGN AFFAIRS
HOUSE OF REPRESENTATIVES

ONE HUNDRED FOURTEENTH CONGRESS

SECOND SESSION

JUNE 9, 2016

Serial No. 114–215

Printed for the use of the Committee on Foreign Affairs

Available via the World Wide Web: http://www.foreignaffairs.house.gov/ or
http://www.gpo.gov/fdsys/

U.S. GOVERNMENT PUBLISHING OFFICE

20–381PDF   WASHINGTON : 2016

For sale by the Superintendent of Documents, U.S. Government Publishing Office
Internet: bookstore.gpo.gov   Phone: toll free (866) 512–1800; DC area (202) 512–1800
Fax: (202) 512–2104   Mail: Stop IDCC, Washington, DC 20402–0001

COMMITTEE ON FOREIGN AFFAIRS

EDWARD R. ROYCE, California, *Chairman*

CHRISTOPHER H. SMITH, New Jersey
ILEANA ROS-LEHTINEN, Florida
DANA ROHRABACHER, California
STEVE CHABOT, Ohio
JOE WILSON, South Carolina
MICHAEL T. McCAUL, Texas
TED POE, Texas
MATT SALMON, Arizona
DARRELL E. ISSA, California
TOM MARINO, Pennsylvania
JEFF DUNCAN, South Carolina
MO BROOKS, Alabama
PAUL COOK, California
RANDY K. WEBER SR., Texas
SCOTT PERRY, Pennsylvania
RON DeSANTIS, Florida
MARK MEADOWS, North Carolina
TED S. YOHO, Florida
CURT CLAWSON, Florida
SCOTT DesJARLAIS, Tennessee
REID J. RIBBLE, Wisconsin
DAVID A. TROTT, Michigan
LEE M. ZELDIN, New York
DANIEL DONOVAN, New York

ELIOT L. ENGEL, New York
BRAD SHERMAN, California
GREGORY W. MEEKS, New York
ALBIO SIRES, New Jersey
GERALD E. CONNOLLY, Virginia
THEODORE E. DEUTCH, Florida
BRIAN HIGGINS, New York
KAREN BASS, California
WILLIAM KEATING, Massachusetts
DAVID CICILLINE, Rhode Island
ALAN GRAYSON, Florida
AMI BERA, California
ALAN S. LOWENTHAL, California
GRACE MENG, New York
LOIS FRANKEL, Florida
TULSI GABBARD, Hawaii
JOAQUIN CASTRO, Texas
ROBIN L. KELLY, Illinois
BRENDAN F. BOYLE, Pennsylvania

AMY PORTER, *Chief of Staff*   THOMAS SHEEHY, *Staff Director*
JASON STEINBAUM, *Democratic Staff Director*

————

SUBCOMMITTEE ON ASIA AND THE PACIFIC

MATT SALMON, Arizona *Chairman*

DANA ROHRABACHER, California
STEVE CHABOT, Ohio
TOM MARINO, Pennsylvania
JEFF DUNCAN, South Carolina
MO BROOKS, Alabama
SCOTT PERRY, Pennsylvania
SCOTT DesJARLAIS, Tennessee

BRAD SHERMAN, California
AMI BERA, California
TULSI GABBARD, Hawaii
ALAN S. LOWENTHAL, California
GERALD E. CONNOLLY, Virginia
GRACE MENG, New York

CONTENTS

SRI LANKA'S DEMOCRATIC TRANSITION: A NEW ERA FOR THE U.S.-SRI LANKA RELATIONSHIP

THURSDAY, JUNE 9, 2016

HOUSE OF REPRESENTATIVES,
SUBCOMMITTEE ON ASIA AND THE PACIFIC,
COMMITTEE ON FOREIGN AFFAIRS,
Washington, DC.

The subcommittee met, pursuant to notice, at 2 o'clock p.m., in room 2200 Rayburn House Office Building, Hon. Matt Salmon (chairman of the subcommittee) presiding.

Mr. SALMON. Subcommittee will come to order.

Members will be permitted to submit written statements to be included in the official hearing record. Without objection, the hearing record will remain open for 5 calendar days to allow statements, questions and extraneous materials for the record, subject to the length limitation in rules.

I would like to begin my remarks by offering my sincere condolences to those who recently lost loved ones and sustained property damage in Sri Lanka and across South Asia due to Cyclone Roanu.

I wish for a speedy recovery for the Sri Lankan people and hope our newly invigorated development relationship that we're going to discuss today can help meet some of the challenges left in the wake of the storm.

Sri Lanka's lengthy and tortuous civil war between the majority Sinhalese and the minority Tamils of the north and east ended in 2009 but the country remains challenged by deep divisions.

Sri Lanka's prior leader, President Rajapaksa, steered the country in an authoritarian direction which included allegations of pervasive human rights abuses, rampant corruption and the failure to follow the rule of law.

In 2015, the Sri Lankan people chose a new path with the election of President Sirisena and Prime Minister Wickremesinghe. There's an opportunity for a new era of democratic reforms and enhanced U.S.-Sri Lankan relations.

Relations between the U.S. and Sri Lanka under the Rajapaksa government were often strained due in part to human rights concerns and the treatment of the minority Tamil population.

We are optimistic that the Sirisena-led government is committed to change and have already begun implementing important reforms. In 2015, the Sri Lankan Parliament passed its nineteenth constitutional amendment to strengthen democratic governance

(1)

and the government co-sponsored a U.N. Civil Rights Council resolution addressing atrocities committed during the civil war.

However, the Sirisena government now appears reluctant to allow foreign judges and prosecutors to participate in war crimes investigations as called for in the U.N. resolution.

President Sirisena has the difficult task of maintaining the government unity that is needed to pass constitutional reforms.

He has found himself between a rock and a hard place and any moves favored by one element of Sri Lanka's political puzzle could alienate another, potentially undermining his political support and breaking the fragile consensus that makes reform even possible.

In light of this challenge late last year, Secretary Kerry announced a U.S. assistance commitment of $40 million to support comprehensive reforms in Sri Lanka, which the administration hopes will have a significant effect on the trajectory of Sri Lanka's democratic reform and reconciliation process.

Closer U.S.-Sri Lankan ties founded in democratic values will facilitate a stronger foundation that will serve as a solid basis for broader cooperation in the Indian Ocean region as well.

Under the Rajapaksa—I apologize, I should have a better handle on that name—leadership human rights became a wedge issue for the United States and Sri Lanka, weakening the relationship, and in response Sri Lanka turned to China for support.

China considers to assert considerable influence, funding development projects in Sri Lanka including the Colombo Port City Project, a $1.4 billion infrastructure project almost entirely funded by Chinese foreign direct investment.

The port is strategically located along the busiest commercial sea lane in the world and will be a key part of China's One Belt, One Road Maritime Silk Road vision to expand its influence by investing in infrastructure along the trade and energy routes that transit the Indian Ocean.

China's regional investments are difficult for small nations like Sri Lanka to pass up. These offers are easy to accept as they do not come with commitments to reform in any way.

Through our increased development commitment and diplomatic ties, the United States is recognizing Sri Lanka's geopolitical significance to the region and I do support this elevated cooperation.

President Sirisena has shown a willingness to work more closely with the United States and in February of this year our nations began the annual U.S.-Sri Lanka partner dialogue, bringing new opportunities for the bilateral relationship.

And I look forward to our panel of experts suggesting ways in which we might enhance the U.S.-Sri-Lankan relationship to our mutual benefit.

I also hope they will share insights on Sri Lanka's delicate politics and make recommendations for the future of the U.S.-Sri Lankan relations.

This is a heightened—there is a heightened sense of optimism surrounding Sri Lanka's recent changes and I look forward to today's hearing to discuss ways we can prioritize those efforts.

And I'd like to turn now to Mr. Sherman for any statements he might have.

Mr. SHERMAN. Mr. Chairman, thank you for holding this hearing and I join with you in concern about China's expansion into the Indian Ocean and especially in Pakistani and Sri Lankan ports.

First, I want to express my sympathy and condolences for all those in Sri Lanka impacted by the flooding associated by Cyclone Roanu. I hope that the hundreds of thousands of people who were displaced can return to their homes and rebuild soon. I'm looking forward to those whose loved ones are missing hopefully being reunited with them.

Last year, Sri Lanka saw some positive developments. I expect there's near universal approval among the subcommittee members for the election of Sri Lankan President Sirisena and the reaffirmation of the decision in the parliamentary elections later in the year.

The elections brought to an end the previous government, which had become increasingly intolerant. These elections represented a true success for the democratic spirit. The new President deserves recognition for reducing the power of the presidency.

I look forward to one day complimenting an American President for scaling back the expansion of the imperial presidency here in the United States.

But returning to Sri Lanka, the new President there has scaled back the powers of the presidency, creating more space for dissent and free expression and opening the country to greater scrutiny by international human rights organizations.

These are notable steps. It's never easy to heal a civil war. The current government came in with a set of promises and impressed the world. Sri Lanka's co-sponsorship in October 2015 of the U.N. Human Rights Council resolution recommending concrete steps toward true political reconciliation was truly and widely acclaimed.

There were promises of the return of land seized during the conflict of accountability with international oversight for those who committed crimes, of constitutional reforms to move power to regions and of changes in the security sector that would end a culture that promoted abuse with impunity.

Last month, I met with the Sri Lankan Ambassador and encouraged Sri Lanka to move forward with plans to continue political reconciliation. The Ambassador described a decline in the military's role and in its presence in the north and east of the country, and the constitutional council's work toward giving more power to local officials.

What I've heard from others, particularly from Tamil groups, is that the political process of reconciliation and security sector reform are not moving forward nearly as quickly as they should.

It is encouraging that the government has established an office of missing persons but we have yet to see how it can operate independently from the government, how it will be resourced and how effective it will be.

The government has promised to reduce the role of the military but the defense budget has actually grown from $1.2 billion in 2009, which is when the conflict ended, to a new higher level of $2.13 billion in 2016.

The government has declared that it will resettle all those displaced in the war by the end of this year. Yet, it has not returned the vast majority of land seized during the conflict.

It is deeply disturbing to learn that both the President and Prime Minister of Sri Lanka have declared their intention to pursue a truth and reconciliation mechanism devoid of international judges. The Tamil population is unlikely to accept this as impartial justice.

Most critical is the issue of the return of government-seized land. The slow progress on this front represents not only a burden on tens of thousands of those who have been displaced, many of whom remain homeless but also a major barrier to building trust between the peoples of north and east Sri Lanka with the central government.

This is a tenuous moment. There is still a sense of optimism, but the government can no longer just rest on this sense of optimism that came with its election.

I look forward to the witnesses' assessment of these processes and especially for direction on what the United States can do to advance full reconciliation between the Sinhalese and the Tamils with due respect for human rights and accountability. Sri Lanka has traditionally been one of the most advanced and prosperous nations in South Asia and I look forward to it also being a beacon of human rights as well, and I yield back.

Mr. SALMON. Thank you.

Just want to advise the committee members and the panelists there's a good likelihood that we're going to be called for floor votes anytime in the next few minutes. So there are other members that would like to make opening statements.

So there's a real good possibility we may end up having to do that and then come back. So I will apologize to the witnesses ahead of time.

Mr. Chabot.

Mr. CHABOT. Thank you, Mr. Chairman.

I want to thank you for holding this hearing and thank the witnesses for being here. As a former chair of this committee, I have taken a particular interest in Sri Lanka and I visited there and been in the northeast and saw the burned-out buildings and a lot of the damage and things which had been caused by a lot of years of war and a lot of lives destroyed.

And just yesterday Sri Lanka acknowledged approximately 65,000 people missing during the 26 years of the off and on civil war. But now 6 years after the official end of the civil war there may be real opportunity to reconcile the people of Sri Lanka and rebuilt this really beautiful country. So I hope that they are successful.

However, I do remain somewhat weary. Although Sri Lanka is in the midst of early signs of actually attaining a sustaining peace and democracy, the scars of the civil war still remain and recently it was somewhat alarming when President Sirisena vowed to eradicate the LTTE ideologies both locally and internationally and I think this kind of rhetoric can be counterproductive but also damaging for the long-term prospects for national reconciliation, which is absolutely critical.

So I know these are exceptionally complex issues. I thank you and commend you for holding the hearing and yield back.

Mr. SALMON. Thank you.

Ms. Meng.

Ms. MENG. Thank you, Chairman Salmon and Ranking Member Sherman, as well as all of our distinguished guests for coming to testify here today.

I especially love to see a professor from City University of New York on our panel. We continue to express our condolences to so many people and their families who have been affected by the landslides and our thoughts and prayers continued to be with them.

The election of President Sirisena in January 2015 brought the promise of a wide variety of reforms and a more inclusive government that would protect the interests of all Sri Lankans regardless of ethnic and religious affiliations.

The United States has a strong interest in ensuring that Sri Lanka remains committed to these reforms and we have certainly deepened our engagement with Sri Lanka in anticipation that a Sirisena government will follow through with these promises.

Sri Lanka has certainly taken some steps to implement a few reforms. But many people, particularly in the minority populations, experience ongoing violence and have been frustrated with the slow reform process that remains extremely vulnerable to political divisions.

I look forward to hearing your assessment on the current reform process and challenges. Thank you, and I yield back.

Mr. SALMON. Thank you.

Mr. Donovan.

Mr. DONOVAN. Thank you, Chairman. I would like to thank Subcommittee Chairman Matt Salmon and Ranking Member Brad Sherman along with their staffs for holding this hearing.

Although I am not a member of this committee, I am grateful for the opportunity to speak here today. The relationship between the United States and Sri Lanka is important to my district of Staten Island and western Brooklyn because I represent the largest population of Sri Lankans in the United States. And welcome, Professor. It is great to have another New Yorker in the room.

Many of my constituents are ethnic Tamils and left Sri Lanka during the civil war that lasted 26 years. They could not have been more relieved when it ended in 2009 and elections were conducted in 2015.

These elections in Sri Lanka have provided an opening for change and reforms that have been taken place. However, I am not sure if the reforms have gone far enough. So U.S. attention and encouragement remains vital.

In particular, the reforms needed for reconciliation between Sinhalese and Tamils, Hindus, Christians, Muslims and Buddhists after a long war have not yet been accomplished.

We need security sector reform to reorient the military for peace time, political reform to provide greater autonomy for regional governments, and legal reform for neutrality of the judiciary and criminalization.

Criminalizing terrible abuses such as enforced disappearances, war crimes and crimes against humanity remain as important tasks for the future.

Sri Lanka has made important commitments in the area of accountability and transactional justice and needs to be held to those commitments in the areas of truth telling, justice, reparations and institutional reforms so that reconciliation can take place.

I look forward to hearing from the witnesses and reporting back to my constituents, and I yield back the remainder of my time, Mr. Chairman.

Mr. SALMON. Thank you. We are proud to be joined today by an esteemed group of panelists—first, Ms. Lisa Curtis, senior research fellow at the Heritage Foundation, welcome; Ms. Kara Bue, partner at Armitage International; and Dr. Nimmi Gowrinathan.

Did I say that right? Close enough, for government work anyway? A visiting professor from the city of New York.

And we are really thrilled to have you each here today and we will start with Ms. Curtis.

STATEMENT OF MS. LISA CURTIS, SENIOR RESEARCH FELLOW, ASIAN STUDIES CENTER, THE DAVIS INSTITUTE FOR NATIONAL SECURITY AND FOREIGN POLICY, THE HERITAGE FOUNDATION

Ms. CURTIS. Thank you, Chairman and——
Mr. SALMON. Oh, thank you.
Ms. CURTIS. Thank you, Chairman Salmon, Ranking Member Sherman, the rest of the distinguished members of the subcommittee, for inviting me here today to talk about U.S.-Sri Lankan relations.

I will summarize my written testimony and ask that my full written testimony is submitted for the congressional record.

Let me join the voices of the members of the panel to express my sympathy for the victims of the severe flooding and landslides that struck Sri Lanka last month. My thoughts and prayers go out to the families of those who lost their lives as well as those who lost homes and other property.

There has been a rapid turnaround in U.S.-Sri Lankan relations in the past 18 months since President Maithripala Sirisena took power. The passage of the nineteenth amendment that curbed the powers of the presidency just a little over a year ago was a milestone on the path back to democracy.

Indeed, the democratic reform process is enabling our countries to improve relations and Sri Lanka continues to be important for its geographic position at the maritime crossroads of Asia and the Middle East.

The results of the parliamentary elections that were held in August 2015 further raised hopes that the country would continue down a path of reform and reconciliation.

Sirisena cooperated with the United National Party in elections that brought Ranil Wickremesinghe to power as the new Prime Minister and the two sides formed a unity government.

In a major departure from the former Rajapaksa government's triumphalist attitude toward the 2009 defeat of the LTTE, the Unity Government in September 2015 co-sponsored a U.N. Human Rights Council resolution acknowledging that war crimes were committed by both the government and LTTE insurgents during the civil war.

In addition to lifting curbs on the media, opening travel to the northern parts of the country, this Sri Lankan Government has also welcomed international human rights organizations to the country, a practice that the previous government shunned.

The cabinet also recently approved the establishment of an Office of Missing Persons, although some members of the Sri Lankan society have complained that they were not consulted about the move.

The government has vowed to adopt a new constitution that abolishes the executive presidency, adopts electoral reform and strengthens provincial devolution.

Despite all of these positive steps, there remains concerns within the Tamil activist community that the human rights reform process is beginning to stall. One contentious issue is whether there will be foreign judges on the panel to investigate human rights abuses.

There is tremendous resistance from the majority Sinhalese nationalists, who still hold a large chunk of parliamentary seats, to the idea of international judges determining the fate of Sri Lankan military officials.

Tamil human rights activists question whether the U.S. is over estimating the level of change at the grass roots level or giving too much credit to the government when there are still major human rights concerns among the Tamil people.

Let me say a few brief words about China and India, and Sri Lanka's relationship with these two key countries. There has been criticism of the Rajapaksa government's cozying up to China and questions surrounding large-scale infrastructure projects that were pursued during his tenure.

Sri Lanka's willingness under the Rajapaksa regime to allow Chinese submarines to dock at Colombo's ports twice in late 2014 alarmed Indian officials, who are wary of China's increasing influence in its back yard.

Sri Lanka has since toned down its relationship with China. However, China will continue to factor largely in Sri Lanka's economic future as Prime Minister Wickremesinghe's recent visit to Beijing demonstrated.

Sri Lanka needs Chinese infrastructure investment and now that the country is facing a financial crunch it cannot afford to alienate China to which it owes $8 billion in debt.

So moving forward, the U.S. should encourage the democratic reform process that is underway, encourage more speedy movement toward reconciliation and transitional justice.

It should build broader economic and investment ties with Sri Lanka and assist with the revitalization—the economic revitalization of the war-torn areas of the north and east.

Without economic and job opportunities, it will be difficult to sustain support for peace and reconciliation.

Lastly, the U.S. should focus on enhancing maritime cooperation with Sri Lanka, recognizing the pivotal position that Colombo occupies in the Indian Ocean region.

So in conclusion, there is a unique opportunity to move forward with ethnic reconciliation and to unify the country following nearly three decades of civil war, and I think the unity government deserves credit for its implementation of democratic reforms.

But there is still a great deal of work to be done in promoting ethnic reconciliation and a durable peace.

Thank you.

[The prepared statement of Ms. Curtis follows:]

"Sri Lanka's Democratic Transition: A New Era for the U.S.– Sri Lanka Relationship"

Testimony before

The House Committee on Foreign Affairs

Subcommittee on Asia and the Pacific

June 9, 2016

Lisa Curtis

Senior Research Fellow

The Heritage Foundation

My name is Lisa Curtis. I am Senior Research Fellow at The Heritage Foundation. The views I express in this testimony are my own and should not be construed as representing any official position of The Heritage Foundation.

I would like to take this opportunity to express my sympathy for the victims of the severe flooding and landslides which wracked Sri Lanka last month. My thoughts and prayers go out to the families of those who lost their lives in the disaster as well as those who lost their homes and other property. The people of Sri Lanka have demonstrated their strength and resilience in the face of terrible natural disasters in the past, and I have no doubt they will overcome this current crisis.

Introduction

There has been a rapid turn-around in U.S.–Sri Lankan relations in the past 18 months since President Maithripala Sirisena took power. Passage of the 19th amendment just a little over a year ago was a milestone on the path back to democracy. The democratic reform process is enabling closer relations between the U.S. and Sri Lanka, whose geographic position at the maritime crossroads of Asia and the Middle East has become more significant with China's rise.

In addition, the Sri Lankan government's decision to co-sponsor a U.N. Human Rights Council Resolution that called for post-war reconciliation and an investigation of alleged war crimes was a promising step, kindling hopes for a genuine accountability process that would help foster national unity and reconciliation. The human rights community noted that the adoption of the resolution could mark a turning point for human rights in Sri Lanka.[1]

However, nine months after the adoption of the U.N. resolution, there is concern that the human rights reform process has stalled, and that the government is squandering an opportunity to reconcile the country and address Tamil grievances in a way that ensures that Sri Lanka will never again become embroiled in civil war.

U.S.–Sri Lankan Relations: A New Chapter

U.S.–Sri Lankan relations have been on an upswing ever since Sri Lankan President Maithripala Sirisena defeated Mahinda Rajapaksa in the January 2015 election. Sirisena defected from Rajapaksa's cabinet and ran against him on pledges to restore parliamentary democracy and rein in corruption. President Sirisena formed a coalition government with the opposition United National Party (UNP) led by Ranil Wickremesinghe and quickly made changes, including lifting media restrictions and allowing foreigners to travel to the war-torn northern part of the country. Five months after Sirisena took the helm, the Sri Lankan parliament passed Article 19 to curb the powers of the presidency by reinstating a two-term limit to the presidency, limiting the president's ability to dissolve parliament, reviving the Constitutional Council, and establishing independent commissions to oversee the judiciary and police.

The U.S. has welcomed Sri Lanka's return to parliamentary democracy. U.S. Secretary of State John Kerry's trip to Colombo in May 2015 shortly after the historical vote to curb the powers of

---

[1] News release, "Sri Lanka: UN War Crimes Resolution Marks a Turning Point for Victims," Amnesty International, October 1, 2015, https://www.amnesty.org/en/latest/news/2015/10/sri-lanka-un-war-crimes-resolution-marks-a-turning-point-for-victims/ (accessed June 6, 2016).

the presidency was the first visit by a U.S. Secretary of State to Sri Lanka in more than 40 years, marking a milestone in relations.

The results of parliamentary elections held in August 2015 further raised hopes that the country would continue down the path of reform and reconciliation. Sirisena cooperated with the UNP in the elections that brought Wickremesinghe to power as the new prime minister. The UNP and Sirisena's faction of the Sri Lankan Freedom Party (SLFP) formed a unity government and signed an agreement to work together to draft a new constitution safeguarding the rights of all ethnic groups. Rajapaksa's alliance, the United People's Freedom Alliance (UPFA), won 95 of the total 225 seats in parliament, leaving him and his loyalists in charge of a powerful legislative bloc.

In a major departure from the former Rajapaksa government's triumphalist attitude toward the 2009 defeat of the Liberation Tigers of Tamil Eelam (LTTE), the new Unity Government led by Sirisena and Wickremesinghe in September 2015 co-sponsored a U.N. Human Rights Council Resolution acknowledging that war crimes were committed by both the government and LTTE insurgents during the civil war. The resolution laid out a path toward a transitional justice process led by Sri Lanka with support and involvement from the international community.

In February of this year, Sri Lankan Foreign Minister Mangala Samaraweera visited Washington to inaugurate the first "U.S.–Sri Lanka Partnership Dialogue." The dialogue focused on governance, development cooperation, and people-to-people ties. The Joint Statement released on February 29, 2016, noted Sri Lanka's "pivotal geo-strategic location within the Indian Ocean Region" and called for strengthening maritime security cooperation. It further expressed U.S. support for constitutional and legislative reforms in Sri Lanka, including the repeal of the Prevention of Terrorism Act, and called on the government to return lands in the north to the original owners (some 64,000 acres reportedly remain under military control).[2] Samaraweera's visit to Washington followed a series of senior U.S. trips to Colombo, including U.S. Permanent Representative to the United Nations Samantha Power in November 2015, and Under Secretary of State for Political Affairs Thomas Shannon last December.

As a further sign of warming U.S.–Sri Lankan relations, the State Department's Directorate of Defense Trade Controls (DDTC) announced on May 4 that licensing restrictions on defense exports to Sri Lanka had been lifted and that it will now review license applications on a case-by-case basis.[3] In 2008, the State Department amended the International Traffic in Arms Regulations (ITAR) to deny licenses for transferring defense equipment to Sri Lanka, except for items related to demining, disaster relief, and aerial and maritime surveillance.[4] The spending bill that included the changes also calls for funding to promote the redeployment and shrinking of the Sri Lankan military now that the civil war has ended.

---

[2] Media note, "Joint Statement from the U.S. Department of State and the Ministry of Foreign Affairs of Sri Lanka on the Inaugural U.S.–Sri Lanka Partnership Dialogue," U.S. Department of State, February 29, 2016, http://www.state.gov/r/pa/prs/ps/2016/02/253775.htm (accessed June 6, 2016).

[3] Jon Grevatt, "Update: US Eases Military Trade Restrictions on Sri Lanka," *IHS Jane's 360*, May 9, 2016, http://www.janes.com/article/60058/us-eases-military-trade-restrictions-on-sri-lanka (accessed June 6, 2016).

[4] News release, "U.S. Eases Military Trade Restrictions on Sri Lanka," Sri Lanka Ministry of Defense, May 9, 2016, http://www.defence.lk/new.asp?fname=us_eases_military_trade_restrictions_on_sri_lanka_20160509_01 (accessed June 6, 2016).

The U.S. also announced in December 2015 that the Millennium Challenge Corporation's (MCC's) Board of Directors had chosen Sri Lanka to be part of a five-year "threshold program." The MCC is an independent U.S. government agency established by Congress in 2004 that provides innovative grants and assistance to countries that demonstrate a commitment to good governance, investments in people, and economic freedom. A senior MCC official said the Sri Lankan program would provide an opportunity for the government to demonstrate its commitment to good governance and policy reform and to consolidate the gains made in these areas in 2015.[5]

In addition to re-establishing parliamentary democracy, lifting curbs on the media, and opening travel to the north, the Sri Lankan government has also welcomed international human rights organizations for visits to the country—a practice the previous Rajapaksa regime shunned. Human Rights Watch visited in October 2015 and Amnesty International traveled to the country in December 2015. The UN Working Group on Enforced or Involuntary Disappearances visited last November for the first time in 16 years. The government has also taken important symbolic steps, such as lifting the prohibition on singing the national anthem in Tamil.

Lifting of media restrictions includes ending censorship of dissident websites and no longer requiring foreign journalists to receive visa clearance from the Defense Ministry. The introduction in parliament in March of the long-awaited Right to Information (RTI) Act also represents a step forward in the reform process. The bill was originally drafted 14 years ago, but Rajapaksa refused to move it forward following his rise to power in 2005. The Act will force public authorities to ensure that citizens have access to information (as long as it does not endanger the country's national security). Dr. Paikiasothy Saravanamuttu, executive director of the Sri Lanka-based NGO Center for Policy Alternatives, said that the RTI Act "could change the way people think of themselves as citizens and accordingly how politicians respond to them."[6]

The cabinet also recently approved the establishment of an Office of Missing Persons, but some members of Sri Lankan civil society complain that they were not consulted about the move, and criticize the government for a lack of transparency in its efforts to establish transitional justice mechanisms.

Finally, the government has stated its commitment to adopting a new constitution that abolishes the executive presidency, adopts electoral reform, and strengthens provincial devolution. The first parliamentary steering committee meeting on the issue was held in early April. The Tamil National Alliance (TNA) supports a federal system of government, while Sinhalese nationalists support preservation of the country's unitary status. Another major question is whether the northern and eastern provinces will be merged, as per wishes of the Tamil community, even though both Muslims and Sinhalese oppose the idea of combining the two provinces. Yet another

[5] "Sri Lanka Threshold Program," Millennium Challenge Corporation, December 2015, https://www.mcc.gov/where-we-work/program/sri-lanka-threshold-program (accessed June 6, 2016).
[6] Ingeborg Lohfert Haslund-Vinding, "The Right to Information Act: Finally a Reality?" Groundviews.org, May 7, 2015, http://groundviews.org/2015/05/07/the-right-to-information-act-finally-a-reality/ (accessed June 6, 2016).

controversial issue is whether the constitution will maintain language that essentially establishes Sri Lanka as a Buddhist state by vowing to "protect and foster" Buddhism.[7]

Steps toward devolution—which lie at the heart of the ethnic question—will be impossible unless the government engages in a major campaign to build public support for the constitutional changes, especially among the Sinhalese population in the south. Many Tamil observers doubt that the government is committed to pushing for such consequential changes, and believe, instead, that the push for constitutional reform may be a whitewash set up for failure.

Momentum Slows

While there has been notable progress on democratic reform in Sri Lanka since Sirisena took power, some of the momentum on establishing a reconciliation process has stalled in recent months. There is a growing feeling among the Tamils that the government has started to drag its feet on setting up a credible domestic inquiry into alleged war crimes that meets international standards. There has been protracted argument about whether there will be international participation in such a panel. There is tremendous resistance from nationalists, who still hold a large chunk of parliamentary seats, to the idea of international judges determining the fate of Sri Lankan military officials.

The question of foreign participation in the accountability process will need to be addressed. President Sirisena and Prime Minister Wickremesinghe have both recently publicly came out against foreign participation in any accountability mechanism, even though the U.S. Ambassador to the U.N. Human Rights Council in Geneva, Keith Harper, has said that Sri Lanka must have foreign judges as part of the process. In late January, Sirisena told a BBC interviewer that he will not agree to foreign judges as part of the accountability process.[8]

Human rights activists also have questioned whether the U.S. is overestimating the level of change at the grassroots level and giving too much credit to the government when there are still major human rights concerns among the Tamil. In April, U.S. Permanent Representative to the U.N. Power said that Sri Lanka has emerged as a "global champion of human rights and democratic accountability."[9] While U.S. officials should encourage the positive steps taken by President Sirisena and Prime Minister Wickremesinghe, they should temper their statements to match realities on the ground and acknowledge that a genuine reconciliation and accountability process will take time.

Foreign Policy

Another notable shift by the Unity Government has been in the country's foreign policy orientation. Already mentioned was the outreach to the U.S. There has also been a marked shift toward better balancing relations between India and China.

---

[7] "Sri Lanka: Jumpstarting the Reform Process," International Crisis Group *Asia Report* No. 278, May 18, 2016, http://www.crisisgroup.org/en/regions/asia/south-asia/sri-lanka/278-sri-lanka-jumpstarting-the-reform-process.aspx (accessed June 6, 2016).
[8] Easwaran Rutnam, "Zeid to Seek Clarity on Role of Foreign Judges," *The Sunday Leader*, January 31, 2016, http://www.thesundayleader.lk/2016/01/31/zeid-to-seek-clarity-on-role-of-foreign-judges (accessed June 6, 2016).
[9] Taylor Dibbert, "Samantha Power Misses the Mark on Sri Lanka (Again)," *The Diplomat*, April 29, 2016, http://thediplomat.com/2016/04/samantha-power-misses-the-mark-on-sri-lanka-again/ (accessed June 6, 2016).

There had been criticism of the Rajapaksa government's cozying up to China and questions surrounding the large-scale infrastructure projects that were pursued during his tenure. The Rajapaksa regime had relied heavily on China for investment and military equipment. During the Rajapaksa years, China became Sri Lanka's biggest donor, provided fighter jets, weapons, and radars to the Sri Lankan military, invested in a major $1.4 billion Port City Project in Colombo, and pledged to invest $1 billion to develop the port at Hambantota. Sri Lanka's willingness to allow Chinese submarines to dock at Colombo's port twice in late 2014 alarmed Indian officials, who are wary of China's increasing influence in its backyard. India fears that Chinese investment in South Asian ports not only serves Chinese commercial interests, but also facilitates Chinese military goals.

Sri Lanka has toned down its relationship with China over the last 18 months. Shortly after his election, President Sirisena pledged to put ties with India, China, Japan, and Pakistan on equal footing—a significant departure from Rajapaksa's pro-China policies. One UNP official went so far as to declare: "We will have a balanced approach between India and China, unlike the current regime, which was antagonizing India almost by its closeness to China."[10] The Sirisena government also put on hold the massive Chinese Port City project, saying it would review the terms of the contract and evaluate how to make the project more transparent.

India warmly welcomed the change in the Sri Lankan regime and the apparent reorientation of its foreign policy. Last March, Indian Prime Minister Narendra Modi was the first Indian prime minister to make a bilateral visit to Sri Lanka since 1987. India recognizes that it is far behind China with regard to investment in Sri Lanka (India has loaned about $1.7 billion to Sri Lanka, compared to China's $5 billion, over the last decade). To enhance bilateral economic ties, India is pushing a new trade pact with Sri Lanka called the Economic and Technological Cooperation Agreement (ETCA). India also has helped Sri Lanka deal with its current balance-of-payments crisis by providing a Reserve Bank of India credit swap worth $1.1 billion.

But China will continue to factor largely in Sri Lanka's economic future as Prime Minister Wickremesinghe's recent visit to Beijing demonstrated. During his visit in February, Wickremesinghe announced the resumption of the Port City Project and welcomed a Chinese proposal to develop a Special Economic Zone (SEZ) in Hambantota.[11] Sri Lanka needs Chinese infrastructure investment, and now that the country is facing a financial crunch, it cannot afford to alienate China, which it owes $8 billion in debt. One of the purposes of Wickremesinghe's visit was to seek a swap of the $8 billion debt in exchange for Chinese equity stakes in Sri Lankan public-sector utilities and infrastructure projects.

The Sri Lankan government will likely maintain robust investment and economic ties with China, while backing away from actions that directly provoke Indian security concerns, such as allowing Chinese submarines to dock at Sri Lankan ports. Nonetheless, India will remain wary of

---

[10] Ellen Barry and Dharisha Bastians, "Sri Lankan President Concedes Defeat After Startling Upset," *The New York Times*, January 8, 2015, http://www.nytimes.com/2015/01/09/world/asia/sri-lanka-election-president-mahinda-rajapaksa.html?_r=0 (accessed June 6, 2016).

[11] Shihar Aneez, "Short of Options, Sri Lanka Turns Back to Beijing's Embrace," Reuters, February 10, 2016, http://www.reuters.com/article/us-sri-lanka-china-idUSKCN0VJ2RX (accessed June 6, 2016).

Chinese strategic intentions toward Sri Lanka and its stated interest in making Sri Lanka a centerpiece of its Maritime Silk Road strategy.

U.S. Policy Recommendations:

As U.S.–Sri Lankan relations continue to improve under the Unity Government, the U.S. should:

Encourage the Sri Lankan government to move more expeditiously on establishing an accountability mechanism that meets the standards of the U.N. Human Rights Council Resolution. While the government's current focus on constitutional reform is welcome, it should not come at the expense of holding accountable those who engaged in war crimes.

Provide legal and technical assistance for Sri Lanka to carry out a credible transitional justice program. The U.S. has much to offer Sri Lanka to encourage unity and ethnic reconciliation, such as technical support and advice on investigating and documenting human rights abuses and developing systems of accountability. The recent cabinet approval for the establishment of the Office of Missing Persons is encouraging, but the international community should reserve judgment until the office produces credible investigations and reports on the circumstances of death of the thousands of disappeared individuals. According to the U.N., there may be as many as 16,000 to 22,000 pending cases of missing persons.

Build broader economic and investment ties with Sri Lanka. Despite its deepening economic ties with China, Sri Lanka continues to look to the West for trade and investment opportunities. The International Monetary Fund's (IMF) recent approval of a three-year Extended Fund Facility (EFF) in the amount of $1.5 billion will help support economic reforms and encourage additional investment and lending. The U.S. must support Sri Lanka's efforts to reform its economy and look for ways to increase bilateral U.S.–Sri Lankan trade, and foster inter-regional trade.

Assist with revitalizing economic development and reform in the war-torn areas. USAID and MCC programs could be helpful in encouraging business development and reviving economic activity in the north and east. Without economic and job opportunities and rehabilitation of the war-torn areas, it will be difficult to sustain support for peace and reconciliation.

Reinstate International Military Education and Training (IMET) programs. The U.S. State Department, with support from the U.S. Congress, should resume IMET assistance to Sri Lanka. These training programs provide an important opportunity to impart American values and build relationships between U.S. and Sri Lankan military officials.

Focus on enhancing maritime cooperation. Sri Lanka occupies a pivotal position in the Indian Ocean Region, and Washington must intensify its naval cooperation with Colombo through increased consultations, training, and exercises. The U.S. should welcome and, if possible, foster closer naval ties between Colombo and New Delhi in order to check Chinese naval ambitions in the region.

Conclusion

With the election of the Unity Government in Sri Lanka, there is a unique opportunity to move forward with ethnic reconciliation and to unify the country following nearly three decades of civil war. The strong support from the U.S. and the positive changes in the bilateral relationship over the past 18 months mean that the time is ripe for progress on this front. While the Unity Government deserves credit for its relatively speedy implementation of democratic reforms, there is still a significant amount of work to be done in promoting ethnic reconciliation and a durable peace.

In addition to encouraging democratic reforms and ethnic reconciliation, the U.S. should pursue a multifaceted relationship with Sri Lanka that includes more robust security and economic cooperation, and acknowledges the increasingly important role that Sri Lanka plays in maintaining security in the Indian Ocean Region.

Mr. SALMON. Thank you.

Ms. Bue.

STATEMENT OF MS. KARA L. BUE, FOUNDING PARTNER, ARMITAGE INTERNATIONAL

Ms. BUE. Thank you, Mr. Chairman and Ranking Member Sherman and the other esteemed members of this committee.

I would like to express my appreciation for your willingness to have me appear here to talk about the future of Sri Lanka. I followed it for some time and I am very grateful for the attention it is getting now.

I too would like to express my condolences to the Sri Lankan people during the cyclone that hit several months ago. I was there at the time and it was devastating to see the harm that was done to the people and their property, but I was very proud too that the United States came forward with additional aid that could help the people who suffered from those storms. So I was very happy to see that happen.

I had been asked to talk about U.S.-Sri Lanka relations. Over the last 15 years there has been an ebb and flow in terms of our engagement there.

With the election of President Sirisena and Prime Minister Wickremesinghe, there really is a new opportunity for engagement. They came into power with a platform of good governance and reconciliation, and together with that they came in with the desire to rebalance Sri Lanka's foreign policy.

What that did was open the door for the United States to engage in a wide range of opportunities for support in Sri Lanka's efforts to finally set the stage for lasting peace and it also allowed us to regain our partnership with Sri Lanka on key issues.

For its part, the Government of Sri Lanka has put forth what anyone would consider a very ambitious agenda. I look at it in terms of five pillars—their ideas about constitutional reform, economic stabilization, addressing the painful war legacy, rebuilding democratic institutions and reestablishing rule of law.

In many ways they have made great progress in the 15, 16 months since they've been in power. Importantly, they have undertaken two ambitious efforts.

One is constitutional reform where they're looking to redraft the constitution, have that presented to the Parliament at the end of the year and then thereafter follow it with a referendum.

The other and perhaps more important was Sri Lanka's agreement at the U.N. Human Rights Council meeting to agree to the resolution on reconciliation and transitional justice. That, I believe, is a historic event, particularly given the history of the Rajapaksa regime.

The other thing I would like to note on the Government of Sri Lanka's part is the tone it has taken with regard to ethnic issues and how different that is from the Rajapaksa regime.

I know some of what they are doing is very symbolic but it has been meaningful to people in Sri Lanka. The national anthem, for example, on Independence Day being sung in Tamil was a very big deal to many Tamils.

I met with Chief Justice Wickremesinghe and he was very moved by that fact. On Remembrance Day, which used to be called Victory Day, they held no parades and that, I think, was a testament to the Sri Lankan Government's intentions with regard to reconciliation.

In turn, for all of this the United States has stepped up its engagement as well. Soon after the elections, they had a number of high-level visits. They developed the idea of a new U.S.-Sri Lankan partnership dialogue. The U.S. was very instrumental at the Human Rights Council meeting.

In terms of the resolution we have increased assistance. Forty million dollars, I believe, is what Secretary Kerry offered during his visit in May 2015 and we engaged a bit on military to military engagement and, of course, are looking at economic opportunities.

Having traveled to Sri Lanka several—at least four times in the last 9 months, I did want to offer some caution in the sense that while we are very excited about how U.S.-Sri Lanka relations are going and the direction they are taking, there are clouds in terms of how the Sri Lankan Government can move forward.

They face a lot of challenges in trying to implement their wide ambitious agenda. The first is that it is very big and it has a lot of moving parts.

For Sri Lanka to do everything it wants to do, it is going to take a long and very complicated process to get things done and I think that is something that everyone needs to realize.

They also lack resources and institutional capacity, both in terms of people and in infrastructure. There are people within the military, within the bureaucracy and within political parties that aren't really on board in terms of what this ambitious agenda is about to do.

So they do face a lot of controversy there and on top of it, the new government is part of a very diverse and unique coalition within the Sri Lankan political party.

So there is a lot left to be done and not everyone has gotten down to work and is attempting to address its agenda. Having talked to people in the north and east, they are not yet feeling the peace dividend.

What I have heard is a statement that is commonly used, which is that everything has changed and yet nothing has changed. And so the government has a lot left to do to respond to the needs of the people in the war-affected areas and that too is a very large challenge and something that we should try to help them with.

In all of this, I think the areas that deserve the most attention are leadership and confidence-building measures. The Sri Lankan Government has a short time frame in which to get a lot done and people in the war-affected areas in particular aren't going to give it that much time before their positions start to harden and, frankly, I think they're already starting to harden.

And so in terms of leadership and confidence building, leadership is the idea of greater communication on the part of the Sri Lankan Government.

In terms of their agenda, I don't think they have done well enough in educating and bringing along all people of Sri Lanka— the people in the south as well as the north and east—in terms of what they are trying to do to respond to everybody's needs. Communication is a big factor.

In terms of confidence-building measures, the idea would try to change the mantra in the north and east about how everything has changed and nothing has changed. Start making things change a little bit for the better in terms of focusing on more land release, for example.

Lastly, an area that I think the U.S. should look at in greater detail is the idea of a donor conference for development in the north and east.

In 2003, after the cease fire had taken place, the United States was instrumental in bringing together an international coalition in a donor conference in Tokyo where they raised $4.5 billion for a period of 3 years.

And that gave people a lot of hope. Now, the rancorous politics in Sri Lanka dashed those hopes and war returned. But in this instance where we feel there is a little more hope and a little more opportunity for lasting peace, I do think it would be wise to consider another type of effort where we could be instrumental making tangible change happen in the war-affected areas.

And with that, I would like to thank you for your time and consideration.

[The prepared statement of Ms. Bue follows:]

Testimony of Kara L. Bue
Founding Partner, Armitage International, L.C.

House Committee on Foreign Affairs
Subcommittee on Asia and the Pacific

June 9, 2016
Subcommittee Hearing: Sri Lanka's Democratic Transition: A New Era for the U.S.-Sri Lanka Relationship

Mr. Chairman, committee members, I would like to express my appreciation for the opportunity to appear before your committee to discuss future prospects for U.S.-Sri Lanka relations.

In 2009, six months after the military defeat of the Liberation Tigers of Tamil Eelam (LTTE) by government forces, the U.S. Senate Committee on Foreign Relations issued a report titled "Recharting U.S. Strategy After the War." It began with a sentence that is equally true today as it was then. "Sri Lanka stands at a critical juncture in its efforts to secure a lasting peace." What is different now, however, is that the odds for securing that lasting peace are somewhat improved.

The presidential and parliamentary elections of 2015 that brought President Maithripala Sirisena and Prime Minister Ranil Wickremesinghe into power have resulted in a paradigm shift away from the authoritarian and chauvinistic rule of former President Mahinda Rajapaksa to a reform-minded era focused on good governance and reconciliation. This shift also has effectively ended Sri Lanka's 10-year self-imposed exile from the international community. The new government has made a concerted effort to reach out to the West for support as it moves forward with its ambitious reform agenda. It is in this context that U.S.-Sri Lanka relations have not only improved over the last year and a half, but stand to broaden in ways that support key interests of both nations and continue to improve the odds for lasting peace.

Per your guidance, my testimony today will focus on U.S.-Sri Lanka relations and opportunities for improved relations under the Sirisena administration.

U.S.-Sri Lanka Relations – Recent Past and Present

Over the course of the last 15 years, the pendulum of U.S.-Sri Lanka relations has swung widely. During the first term of the George W. Bush administration, U.S. engagement with Sri Lanka increased dramatically with the start of a Norwegian-driven peace process in 2001. Factors that worked to further heighten the relationship included: the post-9/11 atmosphere in which there was a concerted interest in confronting terrorism worldwide, the election of a pro-West government led by then-Prime Minister Ranil Wickremesinghe, and the personal interest given Sri Lanka by then-Deputy Secretary of State Richard Armitage.

Through 2004, the U.S. worked to support the peace process and the ceasefire agreement it fostered, increased military and development assistance, and opened other avenues of support such as consideration of Sri Lanka's eligibility for the Millennium Challenge Account. Significantly, the U.S. also brought together the international community in support of a donor conference held in Tokyo in June 2003, during which donor countries and international organizations offered an amount in excess of $4.5 billion USD for 2003 to 2006. A co-chairs process was also initiated in connection with the conference that instituted mechanisms for consultation and coordination of donor support that helped focus the international community's efforts in Sri Lanka at that time.

U.S. support, however, could not diminish the rancor of Sri Lankan politics, and the government of President Chandrika Kumaratunga and Prime Minister Wickremesinghe was voted out in 2004. The following year, then-Prime Minister Mahinda Rajapaksa won the presidential election, ushering in ten years of authoritarianism, corrupt family rule, and a tilt in foreign policy away from the West towards China. As fighting between government forces and the LTTE resumed in 2006, President Rajapaksa oversaw the final stages of the war pursuing a controversial military option to end conflict. Unapologetic for the death and carnage that resulted in the war's final days in 2009, the President viewed his legacy as having "won the war" and did little to reconcile the warring sides in its aftermath.

Between 2009 and 2015, U.S.-Sri Lanka relations focused largely on human rights abuses committed at the end of the civil war. The U.S. welcomed the April 2011 U.N. Panel of Experts Report on Sri Lanka and sponsored U.N. Human Rights Council (UNHRC) resolutions in 2012 and 2013, calling on Sri Lanka to address human rights concerns and foster reconciliation. These and other efforts were met with disdain by the Rajapaksa government, and U.S.-Sri Lanka relations deteriorated further.

By the time of the January 2015 presidential election, there was well-worn concern that the Rajapaksa regime would remain in place. It was especially heartening therefore that opposition candidate Sirisena won the election and did so with the support of a diverse coalition that included Tamil and Muslim minorities. The parliamentary elections in August further supported the mandate for good governance and reconciliation, allowing for a national unity government bringing together President Sirisena's Sri Lanka Freedom Party (SLFP) and Prime Minister Wickremesinghe's United National Party (UNP). Although a national unity government has and will make for difficult politics (especially with continued support by some in the SLFP for Mahinda Rajapaksa), it offers Sri Lanka an historic, if narrow, opportunity to address its many challenges.

Since the elections, progress has been made. The government has taken steps to stabilize the economy and begun to reassert good governance practices within the bureaucracy. The overt military presence in the North and East has been reduced and initial progress in releasing military-occupied land in those areas has been made. Press freedoms have returned, and civil society has gained space for dissent and activism. With the passage of the 19th Amendment, powers of the executive president have been reduced and independent commissions established. The police and the judiciary have also begun to function more independently.

The tone of the government on ethnic issues has also improved. Symbolic gestures such as the singing of the national anthem in Tamil on Independence Day and marking May 19, the day the war ended in 2009, as "Remembrance Day" as opposed to "Victory Day" have received a welcome reception.

Further, the government has embarked on two ambitious endeavors to address the national question and the country's painful war legacy. It has taken on the task of drafting a new constitution, which it hopes to put forward to Parliament by the end of the year and to hold a referendum on it shortly thereafter. It has also agreed to a far-reaching resolution at September's UNHRC meeting, which mandates reconciliation and transitional justice mechanisms, including a special court with international participation. Work has continued since then to meet Sri Lanka's commitments under the resolution, and the government has welcomed the visit of U.N. rapporteurs for torture and independence of judges and lawyers.

These dramatic changes have opened the door for increased engagement by the U.S., and the Obama administration was quick to take advantage of it. It initiated a series of high-level visits to Sri Lanka that included Secretary of State John Kerry, Under Secretary for Political Affairs Thomas Shannon, and Ambassador to the United Nations Samantha Power. In turn, the U.S. received the Sri Lankan Foreign Minister multiple times, perhaps most importantly to preside over the inaugural U.S.-Sri Lanka Partnership Dialogue in which the two countries discussed a wide range of topics that included international regional affairs, economic cooperation, governance and development, and security cooperation.

In other areas, the U.S. announced in May 2015 $40 million USD in assistance to support a wide range of reform, reconciliation, and development efforts. The U.S. military has initiated outreach with visitors from the Pacific Command, as well as the symbolic ship visit to Colombo by the USS Blue Ridge. The U.S., together with international partners, played an important role at the September UNHRC meeting to develop and reach consensus on the resolution ultimately accepted by Sri Lanka. And, work continues on bilateral economic issues such as in the latest round of U.S.-Sri Lanka Trade and Investment Framework Agreement (TIFA) talks held in April this year.

These are only a few examples of the stepped up bilateral engagement that has occurred in the last year and a half, but their pace and broad reach reflect the recent pendulum swing for the better in U.S.-Sri Lanka relations.

U.S.-Sri Lanka Relations – Going Forward

Going forward, however, whatever increased U.S. engagement is afforded by better relations should not be allowed to mask the U.S.'s understanding of the many serious challenges the government faces as it tries to move forward on its broad agenda. While there appears to be consensus and trust building in Colombo among parties and on key matters, including constitutional reform, the view from outside the capital is much different.

In the North and East, a common sentiment expressed is "everything has changed and yet nothing has changed." The fanfare associated with the new government in Colombo has not translated into broad-based, concrete changes in the North and East, as yet.

While residents acknowledge the military's reduced outward presence and the consequent reduction in "fear," they are still are keenly aware of the sheer number of military facilities and personnel that remain in place, and express concerns regarding the military's continued involvement in the economic life of the region, their subtle but continued surveillance of communities, and their presence's potential lasting impact on demographic and cultural erosion.

The slow pace of development in the North and East also has dampened peoples' hope for real change. Land releases are believed to be inadequate (in terms of the speed of releases, the quality of land that is released, and the vast swaths of land that are intended to remain under military control), and funding for development projects, including the mechanisms for release, have been criticized. Lack of tangible, significant progress on the release of political prisoners, the Disappeared, and the Missing also has hardened attitudes toward the government.

These concerns, among others, have led to a growing polarization of civil society. Civil society had worked writ large for regime change. But while this feat was a major accomplishment, there is disagreement and concern about degrees of reform which the new government will be able of delivering. Failure to address a political solution results in some civil society actors not trusting the present structures and refusing to be seen as "colluding" with them (some of whom have been cast as "spoilers" and "separatists"); others are cooperating in good faith for outreach and change from within, believing in the new leadership.

On reconciliation and transitional justice, there is widespread sentiment in the North and East that the government's efforts are solely for the benefit of the international community. Further, the many people and organizations with a role in the process have lead to confusion about who is in charge.

On constitutional reform, there is a strong view that the Prime Minister has moved too fast and established a process that lacks consensus and adequate representation. His public views on the extent of reform also have been conflicting, which has concerned many about whether it ultimately will be sufficient as a political solution.

From the perspective of those in the North and East, the change in government was made possible by the "numerical minority" (i.e., Tamils and Muslims). There is the explicit threat that the government should be more responsive to their needs if it is to retain their support.

With positions hardening outside of Colombo, time increasingly matters. The government must continue to show tangible and regular gains toward its commitments both in Geneva and at home if it is to retain popular and international support. The manifestation of a "peace dividend" for all Sri Lankans is crucial; as too is a national commitment to, and understanding of, the government's broad-based agenda.

In this instance, leadership and confidence building must be priorities.

With regard to the former, the Government of Sri Lanka must find a way to communicate to the public more clearly and consistently about what it is trying to accomplish. The North and East must understand that their needs are being heard and acted upon, and the South must understand why it is in their interest to support the government's efforts, particularly on the issue of constitutional reform. President Sirisena has begun to make statements to Southern audiences about the need for change. But greater outreach is required. Without gaining a national understanding of the government's goals and objectives, the government stands to lose the public's support and any hope of "winning the peace."

Equally important is the need for near-term and concrete confidence building measures that builds trust sufficient to carry the nation through what is going to be a long, complex, and difficult process of peace and nation building. There is a growing loss of confidence today due to the slow pace of reforms. Step to stem this loss are needed. Among many others, these could include increased efforts on land release, the demilitarization of the North and East, and the release of political prisoners without charge.

In both instances, the U.S. is well-placed to encourage and support government efforts.

For the U.S. and the international community writ large, Sri Lanka would benefit from an expansion of its engagement. Presently, the international community is largely focused on the Geneva human rights process. While important, greater economic opportunity and development are both key pieces of any peace dividend and should be supported. Sri Lankan government officials have discussed the need for an international donor's conference for development in the North and East akin to the 2003 Tokyo's Donor Conference. Consideration should be given to such an effort.

I hope the Obama Administration and friends in Congress share this outlook. Thank you again, Mr. Chairman, for the opportunity to participate in your hearing today and to offer these thoughts.

Mr. SALMON. Thank you very much.

Dr. Gowrinathan.

STATEMENT OF NIMMI GOWRINATHAN, PH.D., VISITING PRO-FESSOR, COLIN POWELL CENTER FOR CIVIC AND GLOBAL LEADERSHIP, CITY COLLEGE OF NEW YORK, CITY UNIVER-SITY OF NEW YORK

Ms. GOWRINATHAN. Okay. I imagine you all hear a lot of these panels, a lot of these conversations and I think what comes up over and over again is that there is this disconnect between researchers, between activists, between practitioner and policy makers, and I think one of the biggest disconnects is that policy makers don't understand the ground realities, right.

Obviously, it is difficult for policy makers to do. I think, you know, what a lot of my work—what I would like to testify to is how the policies that are made over here affect the people over there—how the people over there experience these policies.

If you pass materiel support for terrorism law in the United States it affects the resources available to a young girl in the northeast in Sri Lanka.

I think the U.S. policies abroad and particularly, you know, we are seeing this with Sri Lanka, are too often committed to an ideal and this feels sort of intentional to me, being committed to an ideal.

That ideal is usually democracy, which is an important ideal to uphold. But this commitment need not challenge political agendas. If you uphold only the ideal then you don't have to shift political agendas and it is these political agendas by the Sri Lankan Government, by the international community and by the United States that can sometimes sustain and create more conflict.

So in Sri Lanka as elsewhere solutions that are based on ideals are not going to be effective—have not been effective. This is particularly concerning right now because where a solution fails, violence returns, and that is what I think all of us don't want to see happen in Sri Lanka.

So as we consider the progress in Sri Lanka, how do we gauge it? Do we gauge it on policies that reflect an ideal to promote peace or do we gauge it on solutions that create structural change that is required to end violence.

Which way are we measuring these policies in Sri Lanka? And this is a really central question because the people these policies affect can feel the difference between the two.

And so there's four areas that I want to look at here to examine the gap between the people's experiences and the policies that we are examining. And the first is transitional justice.

People have been talking a lot about transitional justice in Sri Lanka. There was a new report out from a group of local scholars in Sri Lanka—legal scholars—and one of the first requirements for transitional justice is that you address both truth and justice. The two have to be done together.

And while the question for Sri Lanka is will the Government of Sri Lanka be willing to dig up mass graves, to find the missing husband of a widow, if that same body becomes evidence for war crimes.

Will there be truth and justice? The ground reports reveal that already the initiatives that have started the Office of Missing Persons are asking victims to choose between the two. Do they want truth or do they want justice?

Another thing that you have to have for transitional justice is confidence-building measures. You have to have the confidence of the people. They have to have faith in state institutions.

The Tamils and other groups are still feeling very intensely the reverberations of past accountability efforts. The women I met in the refugee camps at the end of the war they were well aware that there was a United Nations desk to report sexual violence crimes. Nobody went anywhere near that desk for fear of retribution. The people who testified on lessons learned and reconciliation committee immediately faced harassment by security forces. The Office of Missing Persons has already been found to not consult the victims in any sort of genuine process.

In a recent survey in the northeast found that there is a deep disillusionment and mistrust, and this is important not just as a Sri Lankan state but of the international community. The Tamil population feels that the international community, along with the Sri Lankan Government, abandoned them in 2009. So it is important to recognize that there is a deep mistrust and disillusionment in these areas.

Another need for transitional justice is a memorialization of the dead. Memorializing their dead in the northeast has been criminalized. Not just that, they have removed the spaces of worship.

Slowly you are seeing the destruction of temples and the erection of Buddhist statues where people might memorialize their dead.

For many Tamils I've met recently, memory has no value. The way that they survive is by forgetting. They don't want to answer any more questions because they fear that memory will put their lives at risk.

This is a key problem you're going to face and you have this sort of moment where you have development and accountability processes merging together and what you create is this entrenched victimization where a person exists only by the worst experience that happened to them, where they have access to resources only by articulating the worst thing that's happened to them.

And then militarization—obviously, this demilitarization is one of the biggest issues for all communities in the north and east. To show demilitarization, yes, the government has made the governor of the northeast a civilian and not a military commander. So this is—you know, it is showing something.

But if you talk to the civilians there, there was a civilian I spoke to recently who said you don't need checkpoints anymore—you don't need soldiers.

When you have a context where preschool teachers are recruited into the civilian defense force where the only jobs are military-run hotels and hospitals and vegetable shops and on agricultural farms run by the military, then militarization is complete. Everybody is an informant.

For those who have returned home to some of the land that the government has returned, most of them are living in the shadow of military camps.

They are still immediately adjacent to the very forces that were a part of the atrocities committed in 2009. The military mediates every aspect of civic life in the north and east.

Everything from communal functions to private entrepreneurship. They have even left their mark on the school uniforms of Tamil children.

So this type of deep militarization, I think I would caution here has been used as a model for counter terrorism has been held up as something we should, you know, try to replicate and I think here it is important to note the defeat of the LTTE militarily requires a violation of all established human rights and humanitarian norms.

I don't think this is something we want to replicate. And women, peace and security, which is a critical issue now with the U.N. and here at the U.S. that we put a lot of effort into, a recent survey that I did found that while there has not been as many crimes—the magnitude of crimes against women by the state has decreased—the mode of operating remains the same.

So Tamil women still feel that if there is an act of sexual violence there will be no prosecution for that act. And so I think that what we are looking at—what we have to look at is what is the potential for the resurgence of violence.

We use these words like inequality and alienation and these are things that cause violence. But we always use them in a passive way. They are actually active things that are happening. They are political acts.

There is repressive policies that create inequality. There is populations that are alienated. It is done through political acts and these have a political impact.

So when we look at Sri Lanka and we look at political reform right now, what is the genuine political space available for Tamils? If you're going to gauge democratic transition simply by a regime change that shouldn't be how we're gauging it because you still see the arrest of protest organizers. You still have the Prevention of Terrorism Act in place.

A recent report reveals there are still white van abductions. There are still—the use of torture was noted by U.N. rapporteurs.

So as you've seen in other countries like in Myanmar and other countries in democratic transition, the commitment at a national level to a shift in politics, in political dynamics, does not mean there is a structural shift to include the perspectives of marginalized populations and there has not been a shift in that way.

So I would end by saying that the U.S. should have a cautious approach and the statements and policies should be calibrated by the ground realities.

Things like human rights violations, the loss of faith in state institutions, military occupation, a culture of impunity—these are the drivers of violence.

You cannot have a sustainable peace without addressing these things. So rather than measuring progress against the ideal of democracy in Sri Lanka, are we willing to push for the dismantling of political structures that hold inequality in place?

Thank you.

[The prepared statement of Ms. Gowrinathan follows:]

Witness Statement

"Sri Lanka's Democratic Transition: A New Era in U.S.-Sri Lanka Relations"

Witness Name: Dr. Nimmi Gowrinathan

Title/Organization: Visiting Professor, Director of Politics of Sexual Violence Initiative
Colin Powell School for Civic and Global Leadership, City College

Committee: House Committee on Foreign Affairs

Subcommittee: Subcommittee on Asia and the Pacific

Hearing: "Sri Lanka's Democratic Transition: A New Era in U.S.-Sri Lanka Relations", June 9
2016: 2pm

Introduction

Following the sudden regime shift in January 2015, Sri Lanka became a country in transition, ostensibly trying to rid its democratic institutions of authoritarian practices[1] that caused, and sustained, the decades-long civil war. Since his election, President Maithripala Sirisena has been celebrated for his leadership in opening up space -- space for internet freedom, political dialogue, and popular protest. While these shifts have generated new conversations in a deeply divided society, substantive progress towards a truly inclusive, democratic, state cannot be gauged on dialogue and rhetoric alone.

In October 2015, the Government of Sri Lanka co-sponsored Resolution 30/1 at the UN Human Rights Council and committed to several reforms, including the creation of an accountability mechanism with international support[2] to address *both* the past crimes committed *and* the ongoing culture of violence and impunity.[3] At the time of this hearing, the former has primarily been addressed by statements, without the establishment of judicial accountability structures,[4] and while the *magnitude* of rights abuses has decreased in recent years, the entrenched *mode of operating* by the state and systemic nature of human rights violations remain the same.[5] In key areas of transitional justice, political reform, militarization, and women, peace & security, any potential for meaningful progress and sustainable peace should be assessed on the ability of a particularly policy to address the *structural violence* embedded in state institutions. Using that rubric, the majority of Sri Lanka's steps towards reform are demonstrably inadequate.

---

[1] https://www.washingtonpost.com/news/monkey-cage/wp/2015/01/11/sri-lankas-surprise-political-transition/
[2] UNHRC Resolution 30/1, October 2015.
https://documents-dds-ny.un.org/doc/UNDOC/GEN/G15/236/38/PDF/G1523638.pdf
[3] South Asian Centre for Legal Studies, "Criminal and Humanitarian Approaches to Missing Persons", May 3, 2016.
[4] People for Equality and Relief in Lanka (PEARL), Withering Hopes, May 2016.
http://pearlaction.org/wp-content/uploads/2016/04/Withering-Hopes-PEARL.pdf
[5] UN experts urge Sri Lanka to adopt urgent measures to fight torture and strengthen justice system's independence, May 10, 2016.
http://www.ohchr.org/en/NewsEvents/Pages/DisplayNews.aspx?NewsID=19946&LangID=E#sthash.FzJVvLHL.KTiLd
ZT3.dpuf

Transitional Justice

Several rights observers and legal scholars have stressed the centrality of both *truth* and *justice* in the process of transitional justice,[6] even where the two are at odds with the political agenda of the state.[7] The continued security-based approach to transitional justice in Sri Lanka has handicapped even promising steps towards reconciliation, such as newly established Office of Missing Persons which has, at the outset, "placed before victims an artificial and unfair choice between truth and justice"[8] and has not demonstrated any "genuine willingness to consult the victims."[9]

In this context, obfuscation from Sri Lankan leaders regarding the role of international involvement in the accountability mechanism is particularly unhelpful. Last October at the UN Human Rights Council, Sri Lanka committed to involving international judges, defense lawyers, prosecutors and investigators in creating and executing accountability mechanisms. However since then, President Sirisena and Prime Minister Wickremasinghe have reneged on this key commitment, saying the mechanism will proceed without international judges. Given the Tamil community's consistent demand for an international accountability mechanism, and the report from the UN High Commissioner for Human Rights that Sri Lanka's judicial system is an inadequate avenue for redress, the importance of robust international involvement in the accountability mechanism cannot be overstated. Sri Lanka's pattern of making one commitment to the international community and implementing something different within subsets of its domestic constituency is counter-productive and must stop.

Another element critical to the success of transitional justice in Sri Lanka are the confidence-building measures which restore the faith of the Tamil population in state institutions and justice processes, in order to ensure the non-recurrence of violence. A pervasive fear instilled by the collective punishment of the previous regime has left the Tamil population in the North and East terrified to testify to past atrocities, report ongoing abuses, or request information on missing loved ones for fear of detention or torture. Victims who took the risk to testify before the 2010 Lessons Learnt and Reconciliation Commission faced immediate harassment by state forces following their testimonies. Just last month, the Oakland Institute, a California-based NGO, published a report after Tamil IDPs petitioned the organization for assistance and "urged the Oakland Institute to not publish the names of the signatories because they feared retaliation for contacting an international organization," having received calls from

---

[6] Pablo de Greiff, Observations of the UN Special Rapporteur on the promotion of truth, justice, reparation and guarantees of non-recurrence on the conclusion of his second advisory visit to Sri Lanka (26 January to 1 February 2016).http://www.ohchr.org/en/NewsEvents/Pages/DisplayNews.aspx?NewsID=17029&LangID=E#sthash.JoqwIHQ1.dpuf

[7] Ibid [referencing SACLS report]. See also, https://www.washingtonpost.com/news/monkey-cage/wp/2016/05/18/sri-lankas-bloody-civil-war-finally-ended-seven-years-ago-but-moving-on-from-the-past-is-not-easy/

[8] South Asian Centre for Legal Studies, "Criminal and Humanitarian Approaches to Missing Persons", May 3, 2016.

[9] Letter re: Office of Missing Persons (OMP) to Sri Lanka Ministry of Foreign Affairs from Tamil Civil Society Forum and other organizations and individuals, May 29, 2016.

unidentified numbers threatening their work".[10] Despite ongoing debates on transitional justice in the capital, a recent survey of the population in the North-East reveals ongoing human rights violations throughout the North-East and a continued deep disillusionment and mistrust of the state, particularly amongst Tamils and other minority populations.[11] The continued concentration of power in a central state apparatus which participated in mass atrocities will make the success of any confidence-building measures unlikely.

Political Reform

While Sri Lanka's regime change in itself signified a move towards a democratic transition, political space for dissent, the devolution of power, and the establishment of inclusive political institutions remain an issue under the Sirisena administration. Similar to countries in transition elsewhere, such as Myanmar, public statements and changes in political dynamics at the national level *cannot* be interpreted as structural shifts to include the perspectives of marginalized populations, protecting their civil liberties and political rights.[12]

In Sri Lanka, a key tool for political repression, The Prevention of Terrorism Act[13], used by successive regimes throughout Sri Lanka's history to arrest, detain, and torture dissenters, has not, despite Sirisena's promises, been repealed. Recent reports highlight the constant intimidation of political actors[14] and the continued use of "white van abductions" [15] to silence the voices of citizens and journalists alike. Again, the physical presence of protestors in the North and East expressing their grievances, cannot be mistaken for a commitment to offer a genuine political space for the Tamil population, as protest organizers were arrested and detained as recently as two weeks ago.

Even more worrying is the recent conclusion by the UN Special Rapporteurs on Torture and Independent Judiciaries, that torture is a "common practice"[16] in a system that "may indirectly incentivize the use of torture". The judicial system remains heavily politicized and exclusionary, as Ms. Pinto notes, "the diversity of the population is not reflected in the composition of the judiciary, the Attorney-General's office, the police, or the language in which proceedings are conducted."[17] Sri Lanka's post-independence practice of upholding the Sinhala-Buddhist nature of the state remains consistent, even as the political actors in power change.

---

[10] Oakland Institute, Waiting to Return Home: Continued Plight of the IDPs in Post-War Sri Lanka, May 2016. http://www.oaklandinstitute.org/sites/oaklandinstitute.org/files/SriLanka_Return_Home_final_web.pdf

[11] People for Equality and Relief in Lanka (PEARL), Withering Hopes, May 2016.
http://pearlaction.org/wp-content/uploads/2016/04/Withering-Hopes-PEARL.pdf

[12] International Crisis Group, Sri Lanka: Jumpstarting the Reform Process, May 2016.
http://www.crisisgroup.org/~/media/Files/asia/south-asia/sri-lanka/278-sri-lanka-jumpstarting-the-reform-process.pdf

[13] Recently, UN Special Rapporteur on The Independence of Judges and Lawyers found that the Prevention of Terrorism Act allows for "prolonged arbitrary detention" without charge.

[14] OHCHR Report September 28, 2015

[15] http://groundviews.org/2016/06/01/white-vans-and-unlawful-detention-under-the-pta/

[16] The UN Working Group on Enforced and Involuntary Disappearances has also uncovered underground detention centers below a naval base in Eastern Sri Lanka.

[17] http://www.ohchr.org/en/NewsEvents/Pages/DisplayNews.aspx?NewsID=19946&LangID=E

Militarization & Security Sector Reform

In 2014, five years after the end of the war, over 160,000 mostly Singhalese, soldiers remained in the former conflict zones in the North and East. Progress on de-militarization under the Sirisena regime has been analyzed through the physical markers of armed officials, rather than the deeply entrenched intrusion of the military into civilian life. For example, while the appointment of civilian governors to the Northern and Eastern provinces in place of a military official is a welcome transition, the trend of military control of small-scale businesses (vegetable shops, local hotels), military involvement in civilian activities, and the continued recruitment of civilians into militarized forms of labor[18] has not been reversed. The military's involvement in the North-East has so deeply penetrated the fabric of life that the military runs pre-schools, with Tamil children forced to wear uniforms with military emblems.[19] If demilitarization is the longer term goal, in the interim the Government of Sri Lanka should re-distribute its forces to be proportionately stationed throughout the entire island.

Militarization has also shaped the lived experience of civilians in the North and East in several ways. Even with a diminished number of visible checkpoints, the military appropriated vast swathes of private and public property in the North East during and immediately after the war. Though 3,000 acres have been returned to their owners under President Sirisina, one NGO notes that over 12,000 acres of private land[20] are still being held and over 67,000 acres of state and private land have been appropriated by the military.[21] Over 70,000 Tamils and Muslims remain in Internally Displaced Camps, unable to return to their lands (several in the expanding High Security Zones), while some who have been returned are forced to live in the shadow of military camps or in toxic proximity to coal and other newly established state-run factories.[22]

Sri Lanka continues to be looked to as a model for counter-terrorism,[23] and congratulated by key U.S. figures such as Samantha Powers as being a "global champion for human rights," even as the success of a militarized approach to an ethnic conflict was predicated on violations of human rights that amounted to crimes against humanity.[24]

Women, Peace & Security in the North and East

The context of militarization and impunity highlighted above has led to a particularly challenging situation for Tamil women whose vulnerability is heightened as they live in an environment entirely mediated by military forces. Everything from income opportunities (Civilian Defense Force) to shopping for groceries or walking to school requires a constant interaction with the military.

---

[18] "The Forever Victims: Tamil Women in Post-Conflict Sri Lanka", White Paper, Colin Powell School for Civic and Global Leadership. 2015.

[19] http://www.tamilguardian.com/article.asp?articleid=17840

[20] http://www.cpalanka.org/wp-content/uploads/2016/03/Land-Occupation-in-the-Northern-Province.pdf

[21] http://www.tamilguardian.com/files/File/BTF/Land%20occupied%20by%20Security%20forces%20in%20Northern%20province.pdf

[22] [22] Oakland Institute, Waiting to Return Home: Continued Plight of the IDPs in Post-War Sri Lanka, May 2016. http://www.oaklandinstitute.org/sites/oaklandinstitute.org/files/SriLanka_Return_Home_final_web.pdf

[23] Sri Lanka hosted several conferences on techniques of counter terror, there are new alliances being formed between U.S. Military Institutions, such as West Point, to train U.S. cadres in counterterrorism strategies on the island.

[24] OISL report

My own recent report, which relies on over fifty interviews with women in the North and East has some critical findings on the position of Tamil women. Among them are the allegations of rape by state forces, which have declined since the immediate post-war period, however the deep trauma from this period -- coupled with the complete impunity offered to perpetrators of these crimes -- allows rape to persist as one of the primary concerns of Tamil women.

While some sub-groups of Tamil women are 'particularly vulnerable' to rape (those living near large army camps, the disabled), most Tamil women live with a disturbing spectrum of aggressive sexual behaviors from military personnel. This extends to what one Tamil activist called, "psychological forms of sexual violence, threats of rape and sexual intimidation, through the military that is still there, even if the numbers of personnel have decreased." The pervasive fear of rape, in itself, prevents the mobility of women, limiting their productivity and willingness to participate in any public activity whether social, cultural, or political.[25]

Tamil women have consistently been absent from substantive political or peace-building conversations, a significant oversight as noted by the 2015 UN Sustainable Development Goals which cite the exclusion of women as a detriment to the sustainability of peace.

Role of the U.S. & International Community

The role of the United States in the 'democratic transition' is vital. While it has been a leader in the pressure which led to a shift in regime, continued pressure is required to see structural changes that will see the country through a transitional period to a genuine democracy.

- Going forward, the U.S. must take a more cautious approach—while noting progress by Sri Lanka, the broad commendation for statements and small steps detracts from areas where pressure by U.S. and international community has gotten victims some attention –but attention alone is not enough to ensure justice and equality (for example, see comments from new ICG report at pp. 28-29). Statements from the US government must be calibrated based on conditions on the ground, and particularly the North-East, which has borne the brunt of decades of war.

- As the U.S. connections to the North-East, it must be mindful of the military mediation, as it ensures the victim/survivor community has opportunities to engage with the international community and to ensure the international community's evaluation of Sri Lanka's progress on its pledges are appropriately fact-based.

- The U.S. should foreground the cessation of human rights violations, press for the release of military-occupied land, the release of Tamil political detainees, the resettlement of IDPs and, most critically, the demilitarization of the North-East.

- The U.S. and International Community should push the Sri Lankan government to communicate the need for accountability to Sinhala populace as well— the government's own statement that

---

[25] "The Forever Victims: Tamil Women in Post-War Sri Lanka", White Paper, Colin Powell School for Civic and Global Engagement. 2015.

the Channel 4 films depicting horrific war crimes are authentic is a step in the right direction, but this acknowledgement must translate to a broader educational campaign regarding the breadth of abuse the Tamil community has suffered. This is an important step that is undermined by ongoing references to military as "war heroes", which limits the potential for democratic transition in a "Victor's Peace".

- As numerous authorities have noted, Sri Lanka by itself does not have the capacity to deal with the scale of crimes committed during and after the war and would be well-advised to call on outside expertise to deal with these serious breaches of the laws of war and international law. The US has assisted in similar circumstances in other parts of the world.

- The US should keep in place the effective regime of incentives and disincentives that have worked well in the past until significant reforms are in place and working effectively. For instance, restrictions on military aid, licensing and training, should remain until major security sector reform has been accomplished.

Mr. SALMON. Thank you.

With our truncated time for questions and the fact that we are going to be called for votes very soon, if members could maybe hold their questions to 2 minutes.

So anybody that wants to try to get a question in before we leave I am going to adjourn when the votes are called. And I am going to allocate my time to our guest member, Mr. Donovan. So you go ahead and start the questioning and then I will go to the ranking member.

Mr. DONOVAN. I appreciate it, Mr. Chairman. Thank you very much.

I am curious—why do you think the judicial process is so slow? Over 200 Tamils held under these same laws at this moment 7 years after the war has ended. Like, why do you believe that this process is so slow for these individuals?

Anyone, yeah.

Ms. BUE. Well, I can't say for sure exactly why it is so slow. But my understanding is that this is a legacy issue from the Rajapaksa era. There are elements within the government that have been resistant to moving faster on the release of political prisoners.

In speaking with the current government, there are efforts to move past that. I know that they have released some prisoners as of last year and they are looking to release more.

Mr. DONOVAN. Is it true that some of the names aren't even released yet?

Ms. BUE. Yes.

Mr. DONOVAN. I am sorry. I didn't want to cut you off.

Ms. BUE. Oh, no. But yes.

Mr. DONOVAN. Can the United States do anything about this? What is the United States' role here as people back home see?

Ms. GOWRINATHAN. I would say that one of the key things to look at is the role of, again, the military. A number of the cases—when you have the entrenched military in a number of these areas the military is mediating everything.

So what if someone reports a case? What language it's reported in, who they see going into a courtroom? You know, there is—there is sort of an impact on anybody who tries to engage in the judicial process.

I have met—a former ex-combatant I met last year who said that she has five or six pending cases against her by the military for things like throwing away her cell phone because she didn't want to be tracked.

So when the courts are filling up with these types of surveillance cases against all of the Tamils who they suspect to be linked in some way to the Tigers, when women can't walk outside because they have five different cases pending against them by the military, there is not going to be room for the Tamil population to address their grievances within the same court system that came from within a state that controlled the entire judicial mechanisms that appointed all of the Supreme Court judges.

So that, I think, where those two sort of come up against each other you see this constant sort of slowness of the process.

Mr. DONOVAN. Right. And so—and this will be my last question because I want the other members speak because the chairman said we have to run and vote momentarily—the United States' role here—besides suggesting, trying to influence, trying to persuade corrections in this system that you just described as so wrong, is there a role here for the United States besides just as an advisor of telling people this—what you are doing here is wrong and that the effects on women, as you just spoke about, are something that the United States disapproves of.

Just disapproving it is not going to get this to move any further along in the process. What is our role here?

Ms. CURTIS. Well, I think the U.S. has a role in both the private statements it makes to the government but also public statements, to put a little public pressure.

You know, these things are very difficult. You may have parts of the government that want to move forward quickly. But there are political considerations that they have.

So I think they do need our nudging. As I spelled out in my testimony, there have been many positive steps by this government.

But the only way the process will continue to move forward is probably through U.S. and other pressure. So I think it is important for us to make public statements also through the U.N.

The U.N. is meeting today on these issues. So I think working through the U.N. process and continuing to press for concrete and substantive movement, such as releasing political prisoners, it's absolutely necessary for the U.S. to push.

Otherwise, the default will be to move slowly and not take those very difficult steps.

Mr. DONOVAN. Thank you.

Thank you, Mr. Chairman. I yield back.

Mr. SALMON. Thank you. Mr. Sherman.

Mr. SHERMAN. Thank you.

Doctor, the government has sped up a special assembly effort to draft a new constitution. It's expected to grant Tamils regional political power.

Where do things stand now on drafting these constitutional provisions and what is the likelihood that Tamils in the north and east will have some degree of regional authority?

Ms. GOWRINATHAN. The likelihood, I would say, of the devolution of power has always been something that seems very optimistic for the north and east.

You know, the concern, I think, becomes who is mediating that political conversation. So when you have a context where there was a political movement that was articulating the political demands of the people and that shifts to a political party, that may not be as sort of entrenched in the ground realities as you would want.

For me, the concern becomes how do you get the everyday sort of citizen to engage in politics in a way that their opinions come across without being mediated.

And so when you see things like mass protests that is encouraging. Mass protests about the disappeared—mass protests about the missing persons—those are encouraging. But when you see the protestors arrested and harassed right afterwards then again you feel that that space is not a genuine space offered.

It is sort of the streets have opened up and there's less checkpoints but the people are still harassed.

Mr. SHERMAN. Let me try to squeeze in one more question. What is—how is—what signs are there that the government is really going to transfer land from the military back to the people and how much land does the military control in the north and east?

Ms. Bue and then——

Ms. BUE. My understanding is that as for the north there are over 12,000 acres that the military still maintains.

Now, I should have prefaced that by the fact that there are a lot of different numbers floating around. That's just the one that I use.

Mr. SHERMAN. Let me—let me ask the—is—because I have heard a lot about the military-held land. Are we talking here about 12,000 rural acres? Or are we talking about more land than that?

Ms. GOWRINATHAN. They hold a lot more than that and I think there is private and public land that is being held, and I was there last year for this very sort of fancy military ceremony of releasing tiny plots of land to people.

The military still controls a large amount of land in the north and east that should be for—I mean, you still have tens of thousands of internally-displaced people because their homes are in high security zones.

So the lands are still being held by the military and let's say that even where they say formally this is public land but we are going to use it for a base, we are going to use it for a military hospital, we are going to use it for a military-run hotel, that is still occupation of private lands that belong to Tamils.

Mr. SALMON. I thank the panel members for coming today. We appreciate your commitment to improving the lives of people in the region and I think we've had a great discussion. I think it is clear that the U.S. Congress is very interested in moving forward and not just on paper but in reality.

I really appreciate all the comments, and, without objection, the hearing will be adjourned.

[Whereupon, at 2:47 p.m., the Subcommittee was adjourned.]

APPENDIX

SUBCOMMITTEE HEARING NOTICE
COMMITTEE ON FOREIGN AFFAIRS
U.S. HOUSE OF REPRESENTATIVES
WASHINGTON, DC 20515-6128

Subcommittee on Asia and the Pacific
Matt Salmon (R-AZ), Chairman

June 7, 2016

TO: MEMBERS OF THE COMMITTEE ON FOREIGN AFFAIRS

You are respectfully requested to attend an OPEN hearing of the Committee on Foreign Affairs, to be held by the Subcommittee on Asia and the Pacific in Room 2200 of the Rayburn House Office Building (and available live on the Committee website at http://www.ForeignAffairs.house.gov):

DATE: Thursday, June 9, 2016

TIME: 2:00 p.m.

SUBJECT: Sri Lanka's Democratic Transition: A New Era for the U.S.-Sri Lanka Relationship

WITNESSES: Ms. Lisa Curtis
                 Senior Research Fellow
                 Asian Studies Center
                 The Davis Institute for National Security and Foreign Policy
                 The Heritage Foundation

                 Ms. Kara L. Bue
                 Founding Partner
                 Armitage International

                 Nimmi Gowrinathan, Ph.D.
                 Visiting Professor
                 Colin Powell Center for Civic and Global Leadership
                 City College of New York
                 City University of New York

By Direction of the Chairman

The Committee on Foreign Affairs seeks to make its facilities accessible to persons with disabilities. If you are in need of special accommodations, please call 202/225-5021 at least four business days in advance of the event, whenever practicable. Questions with regard to special accommodations in general (including availability of Committee materials in alternative formats and assistive listening devices) may be directed to the Committee.

COMMITTEE ON FOREIGN AFFAIRS

MINUTES OF SUBCOMMITTEE ON _____ *Asia and the Pacific* _____ HEARING

Day___ *Thursday*___Date_____ *June 9, 2016*____Room_____ *2200*____

Starting Time ____*2:00*____Ending Time ____*2:47*____

Recesses |___| (____to ____) (____to ____) (____to ____) (____to ____) (____to ____) (____to ____)

Presiding Member(s)

Salmon

Check all of the following that apply:

Open Session ☑ Electronically Recorded (taped) ☐
Executive (closed) Session ☐ Stenographic Record ☐
Televised ☐

TITLE OF HEARING:

Sri Lanka's Democratic Transition: A New Era for the U.S.-Sri Lanka Relationship

SUBCOMMITTEE MEMBERS PRESENT:

Chabot
Sherman, Meng, Bera, Connolly

NON-SUBCOMMITTEE MEMBERS PRESENT: *(Mark with an * if they are not members of full committee.)*

Donovan

HEARING WITNESSES: Same as meeting notice attached? Yes ☑ No ☐
(If "no", please list below and include title, agency, department, or organization.)

STATEMENTS FOR THE RECORD: *(List any statements submitted for the record.)*

TIME SCHEDULED TO RECONVENE _____
or
TIME ADJOURNED ____*2:47*____

_____
Subcommittee Staff Director